D1257892

ANIMAL SUPERPOWERS

WOOD FROGS
Back from the Dead!

Emma Carlson Berne

PowerKiDS press.

New York

Published in 2014 by The Rosen Publishing Group, Inc.
29 East 21st Street, New York, NY 10010

First Edition

Editor: Joanne Randolph
Book Design: Kate Vlachos

Photo Credits: Cover Michael S. Quinton/National Geographic/Getty Images; p. 5 Gerald A. DeBoer/Shutterstock.com; p. 6 Gary Meszaros/Photo Researchers/Getty Images; p. 7 (sidebar) Carolina K. Smith MD/Shutterstock.com; p. 7 MustafaNC/Shutterstock.com; p. 8 © iStockphoto.com/Giovanni Banfi; p. 9 Chris Hill/Shutterstock.com; p. 10 Cary Anderson/Aurora/Getty Images; pp. 12–13 Francis Bossé/Shutterstock.com; p. 14 Cheryl A. Meyer/Shutterstock.com; p. 15 Marques/Shutterstock.com; p. 16 Sven Zacek/Oxford Scientific/Getty Images; p. 17 JamesChen/Shutterstock.com; pp. 18, 20, 21 George Grall/National Geographic/Getty Images; p. 19 Dr. Gilbert Twiest/Visuals Unlimited/Getty Images; p. 20 (sidebar) Steve Byland/Shutterstock.com; p. 22 John Cancalosi/Peter Arnold/Getty Images.
Interactive eBook Only: p. 7 Francis Bossé/Shutterstock.com; p. 9 MarkMirror/Shutterstock.com; p. 11 Joe McDonald/Visuals Unlimited/Getty Images; p. 15 Sons of Thunder Enterprises Inc/Image Bank Film/Getty Images; p. 17 vesperstock/iStockfootage/Getty Images; p. 18 Natalie Kauffman/First Light/Getty Images; p. 21 (used in graphic organizer) Photo Researchers/Getty Images; p. 22 Mirec/Shutterstock.com; p. 22 Michael P. Gadomski/Photo Researchers/Getty Images.

Library of Congress Cataloging-in-Publication Data

Berne, Emma Carlson.
   Wood frogs : back from the dead! / by Emma Carlson Berne. — 1st ed.
      p. cm. — (Animal superpowers)
   Includes index.
   ISBN 978-1-4777-0751-7 (library binding) — ISBN 978-1-4777-0843-9 (pbk.) — ISBN 978-1-4777-0844-6 (6-pack)
   1. Wood frog—Juvenile literature. 2. Wood frog—Conservation—Juvenile literature. I. Title.
   QL668.E27B47 2014
   597.8'9—dc23
                              2012048579

Manufactured in the United States of America

CPSIA Compliance Information: Batch #S13PK6: For Further Information contact Rosen Publishing, New York, New York at 1-800-237-9932

Contents

What a Frog!

Imagine a person sitting outside all winter long. This person might die of the cold. What if there was an animal that could live with half its body frozen, though? What if there was some superpowered animal that could make its own antifreeze and survive winters, even those near the **Arctic Circle**? There is such an animal. It is the wood frog.

The wood frog is an extraordinary **amphibian** that lives in the forests of North America. It waits out long northern winters semifrozen, then revives in early spring and hops to the nearest pond to lay thousands of eggs. Let's explore the world of the wood frog in the chapters that follow.

This small brown frog may not look like it has superpowers, but it can withstand long winters with its body mostly frozen. Lesser creatures would die in these conditions!

Small, Brown, and Camouflaged

If you were walking in the woods, you would probably have a hard time spotting a wood frog. This little creature is only about 2 inches (5 cm) long. Its skin is a mixture of brown, tan, and olive green, with a black streak over its eyes. It is the perfect disguise for blending into the forest floor. It has two long, powerful jumping legs behind and two short, delicate legs in the front.

The wood frog is known for the black mask on its face. This is an easy way to tell whether you are looking at a wood frog or some other kind of frog.

FROZEN FROG

Most frogs **hibernate** at the bottoms of ponds or underground during the winter but not the wood frog. This little creature just burrows under logs or leaves in the forest. The wood frog can do this because it can survive with up to 65 percent of its bodily **fluids** turned to ice.

Wood frogs spend some time in the water, especially when it is time to lay eggs. Can you see the frog's long back legs and its bulging eyes here?

The wood frog's bulging eyes stick up from the top of its head, as do most frogs' eyes. This way, the frog can see in almost all directions, all the better to catch insects to eat!

Northern Natives

Wood frogs love the cold. They can live farther north than any other reptile or amphibian in North America. The wood frog is also the only frog that lives within the Arctic Circle. However, wood frogs can live in warmer areas, too.

Where Wood Frogs Live

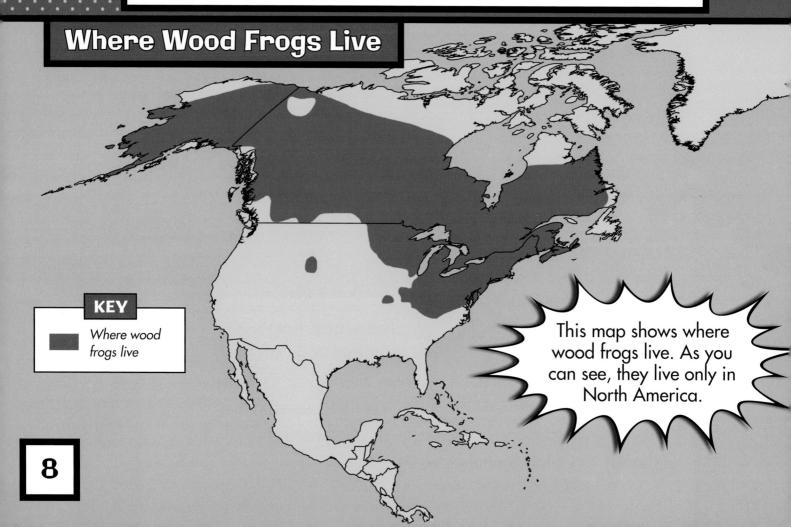

KEY

Where wood frogs live

This map shows where wood frogs live. As you can see, they live only in North America.

Wood frogs live mainly in woodlands and swamps. They can be hard to spot because their coloring helps them blend in with their surroundings.

In fact, their **range** is over 4 million square miles (10 million sq km). It runs all the way from northern South Carolina, up the East Coast, and all through Canada.

Wood frogs almost always live on land, in the woods or swamps. They like cool, moist soil. When they are **breeding**, wood frogs look for **vernal pools** in which to lay their eggs.

The wood frog has the amazing ability to live with more than half its body frozen. This **adaptation** is the only way it can survive long winters in the north. To do this, wood frogs make their own antifreeze out of special proteins and a substance called **glucose**.

A wood frog can also stop its own circulation and breathing. The wood frog sits quietly through the winter months, buried under leaves, with its heart and lungs at rest and its body half frozen. Then in the spring, the wood frog senses the warmer temperatures. Its heart and lungs start up, it thaws, and active life begins again.

This wood frog is just hiding, but come winter, it will burrow more deeply under the leaves, shut down its circulation and breathing, and wait for the spring thaw.

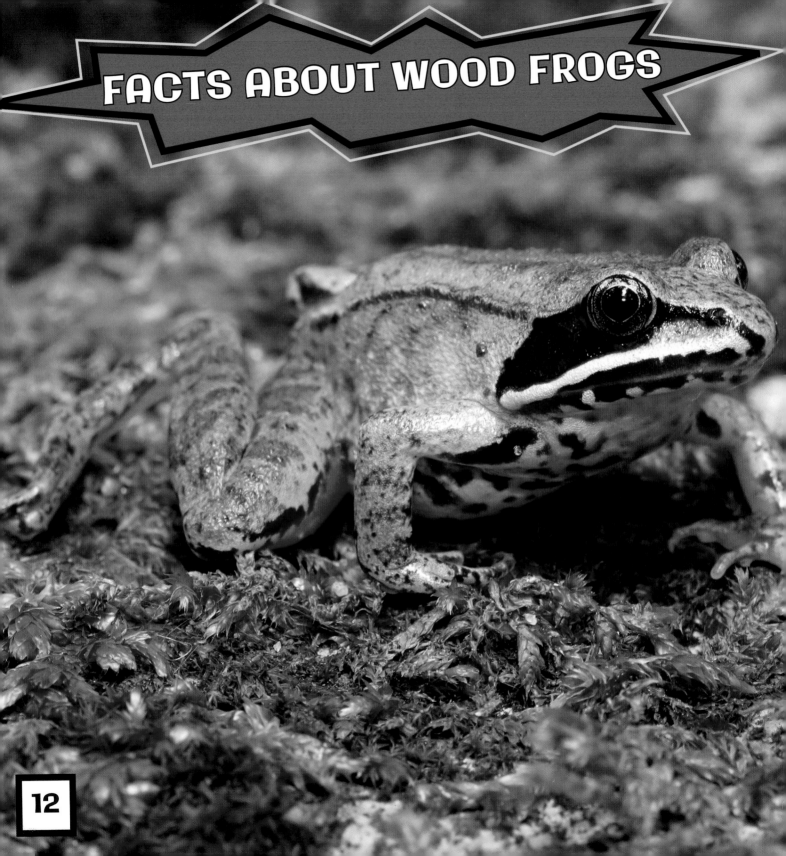

1

Wood frogs come out from hibernation much sooner than other frogs, sometimes as early as February.

2

Wood frogs become full adults, able to breed, between the ages of one and two. They live to be only about three years old.

3

The song of the wood frog sounds very much like a duck quacking. It is also very quiet. A person can hear it only from about 8 feet (2 m) away.

4

Even wood frog eggs can survive the winter in a frozen pool of water. The eggs just stop developing until spring.

5

In a huge mass of **tadpoles**, all from different mothers, a wood frog tadpole can tell which are its own brothers and sisters.

6

Wood frogs that live in Alaska or above the Arctic Circle grow from tadpoles to frogs faster than other frog species because the summers are so short.

Earthworms for Dinner, Anyone?

Slugs are a favorite meal of the wood frog.

If a wood frog had to choose a perfect meal, it might pick a serving of delicious slugs, followed by a nice helping of flies. For dessert, it might munch on some earthworms.

Wood frogs just love insects, worms, and grubs of all sorts. They will eat almost anything they can catch, including beetles, spiders, moth larvae, and snails.

Wood frog tadpoles like to eat rotting plants and **algae**. Sometimes, the tadpoles also have snacks of toad eggs and tadpoles if they happen to find them in the same pool.

Wood frogs are not picky eaters. They will eat pretty much any creepy-crawly creature they can catch, including beetles like this one.

15

It's a Tough World

As much as wood frogs like to eat insects, the little frogs are also a favorite meal for many other animals. When they are in their breeding pools, they're often eaten by water snakes, snapping turtles, and herons. Skunks, raccoons, foxes, and coyotes can easily snap up wood frogs if they find them.

Owls will catch and eat wood frogs if they find them.

Raccoons are omnivores, which means they will eat most anything, including wood frogs!

Snakes, turtles, large insects, and even other frogs and toads often eat the eggs and tadpoles. In fact, so many wood frogs get sick, starve, or are eaten by **predators**, that only about 13 percent of adults survive each year.

Lots and Lots of Eggs

Each spring, wood frogs hop through the woods to vernal pools. In the water, the male frog calls to the female frog. Once two frogs decide to become **mates**, the female frog releases eggs into the water. As she does, the male frog **fertilizes** them.

Vernal pools are quite the place to be in the spring. Hundreds of frogs may gather in a single pool.

The female lays as many as 3,000 eggs in a big, jellylike mass. The mass is generally attached to sticks or grasses in the pond. Other wood frogs lay their eggs nearby. Some small pools can look like they are entirely covered with egg masses by the time the wood frogs are done.

These wood frog eggs will hatch soon. Do you see the dark shape inside the clear egg? When wood frogs hatch, they have thousands of brothers and sisters in the pool with them.

19

From Tadpoles to Frogs

The eggs sit quietly in the pond for about 10 to 30 days. Then tiny tadpoles hatch. They have only heads and tails and look like small fish. The tadpoles eat the jelly from the egg mass. Later, they eat plants in the pond. Sometimes they also eat each other's tails.

There are thousands of wood frog tadpoles in this vernal pool. Tadpoles are a favorite snack of many animals, so there have to be a lot of them to make sure some survive.

DID I HEAR A DUCK OR A FROG?

The wood frog makes a sound like a quacking duck by **inflating** sacs on its shoulders. These sacs look like large peas. The frog inhales air through its nostrils. Then it pumps the air back and forth over its **vocal cords.** The frog's shoulder sacs vibrate and project the sound.

After about 6 to 15 weeks, the tadpoles start **metamorphosis**. Their tails slowly disappear and they sprout legs. Soon, they look like adult frogs, except for a small stump of tail. When they are in their adult form, and their watery home begins to dry up, the new frogs hop away into the forest.

Wood frogs in the froglet stage start to look more like frogs and less like fish. They still have tails at this stage, though.

21

Helping Wood Frogs

Wood frogs have to have vernal pools to live. These small pools exist only in wooded areas. As more and more woods are cut down for houses, offices, or shopping centers, the frogs lose their breeding places.

Wood frogs also make more babies when their pools are in big stretches of forest, instead of little, broken-up sections of woods. By protecting our forests, we can also help these small, superpowered frogs **thrive**.

People are taking over the places where wood frogs live and breed. What can you do to help wood frogs?

Glossary

adaptation (a-dap-TAY-shun) A change in an animal that helps it live.

algae (AL-jee) Plantlike living things without roots or stems that live in water.

amphibian (am-FIH-bee-un) An animal that spends the first part of its life in water and the rest on land.

Arctic Circle (ARK-tik SUR-kul) A pretend circle around the North Pole.

breeding (BREED-ing) Making babies.

fertilizes (FUR-tuh-lyz-ez) Puts male cells together with female cells to make babies.

fluids (FLOO-idz) Liquids.

glucose (GLOO-kohs) The sugar that the body uses for energy.

hibernate (HY-bur-nayt) To spend the winter in a sleeplike state.

inflating (in-FLAYT-ing) Filling with air.

mates (MAYTS) Partners for making babies.

metamorphosis (meh-tuh-MOR-fuh-sus) A complete change in form.

predators (PREH-duh-terz) Animals that kill other animals for food.

range (RAYNJ) The area of land or water where a species of animal might live.

tadpoles (TAD-pohlz) Baby frogs or toads that look like fish and live under the water.

thrive (THRYV) To be successful or to do well.

vernal pools (VER-nul POOLZ) Small ponds that have water only part of the year, have no streams flowing in, and have no fish.

vocal cords (VOH-kul KORDZ) Two small bands of body tissue that stretch across the voice box and move to make sounds.

Index

Websites

Due to the changing nature of Internet links, PowerKids Press has developed an online list of websites related to the subject of this book. This site is updated regularly. Please use this link to access the list:
www.powerkidslinks.com/asp/wfrog/